INTERIOR DESIGN
RAUMGESTALTUNG
DESIGN D'INTERIEURS
INTERIEURARCHITECTUUR

Edited by Macarena San Martín

Art director:
Mireia Casanovas Soley

Editorial coordination:
Catherine Collin

Project coordination:
Macarena San Martín

Texts:
Macarena San Martín

Layout:
Claudia Martínez Alonso

Translations:
Britta Schlaghek (German), Lydia de Jorge (English), David Lenoir (French), Els Thant (Dutch)

Editorial project:
2007 © LOFT Publications l Via Laietana, 32, 4.º, Of. 92 l 08003 Barcelona, Spain
Tel.: +34 932 688 088 Fax: +34 932 687 073 l loft@loftpublications.com l www.loftpublications.com

ISBN 978-84-96936-04-1   Printed in China

INTERIOR DESIGN

RAUMGESTALTUNG
DESIGN D'INTERIEURS
INTERIEURARCHITECTUUR

Edited by Macarena San Martín

KOLON

„Wir lernen die Menschen nicht kennen, wenn sie zu uns kommen; wir müssen zu ihnen gehen, um zu erfahren, wie es mit ihnen steht."

Johann Wolfgang von Goethe, deutscher Dichter und Dramatiker

"To really know someone, you must visit their home."

Johann Wolfgang von Goethe, German poet and playwright

« Pour connaître les gens, il faut aller chez eux. »

Johann Wolfgang von Goethe, poète et dramaturge allemand

"Wil je iemand leren kennen, leer dan eerst zijn huis kennen."

Johann Wolfgang von Goethe, Duitse dichter en dramaturg

Das Wohnzimmer ist ein Ort des Zusammentreffens, der Entspannung und der Freizeit. Mit der Zeit haben sich die Elemente, aus denen es sich zusammensetzt, wie auch die Modetendenzen und persönlichen Geschmäcker verändert. Heutzutage neigt man zu minimalistischeren Räumen und meidet Überladenheit.

The living room is the space designated for reunions, recreation and resting. With the passing of time, its elements have changed, as have tendencies and personal tastes. The tendency today is for minimalist spaces instead of clutter.

WOONKAMERS

Le salon est l'espace destiné aux réunions, au repos et au loisir. Avec le temps, les éléments qui le composent ont changé, comme les tendances ou les goûts personnels. Aujourd'hui, on tend vers des espaces minimalistes plutôt que très chargés.

Een zitkamer is bestemd voor samenzijn, rust en ontspanning. De elementen van een zitkamer zijn in de loop van de tijd veranderd, net als trends of persoonlijke smaken. Vandaag de dag neigt men naar minimalistische in plaats van al te volle ruimtes.

In sehr großen Räumen, oder in denen Weißtöne dominieren, ob bei Wänden, Boden oder Möbeln, empfiehlt es sich, zumindest Teile des Bodens mit einem Teppich abzudecken, da so ein wärmeres, gemütlicheres Ambiente entsteht.

In very large spaces where the color white predominates throughout the walls, floors or furniture, the use of area rugs is highly recommended. This not only provides warmth but it makes the space cozier.

Dans les très grands espaces, où domine le blanc, que ce soit sur les murs, les sols ou les meubles, on conseille de recouvrir au moins une partie du sol d'un tapis qui apporte de la chaleur et rend la pièce plus accueillante.

In grote ruimtes, waar wit overheerst, zowel op de muren en vloeren als in de meubels, is het raadzaam een deel van de vloer met tapijt te bedekken, want dit maakt het warmer en gezelliger.

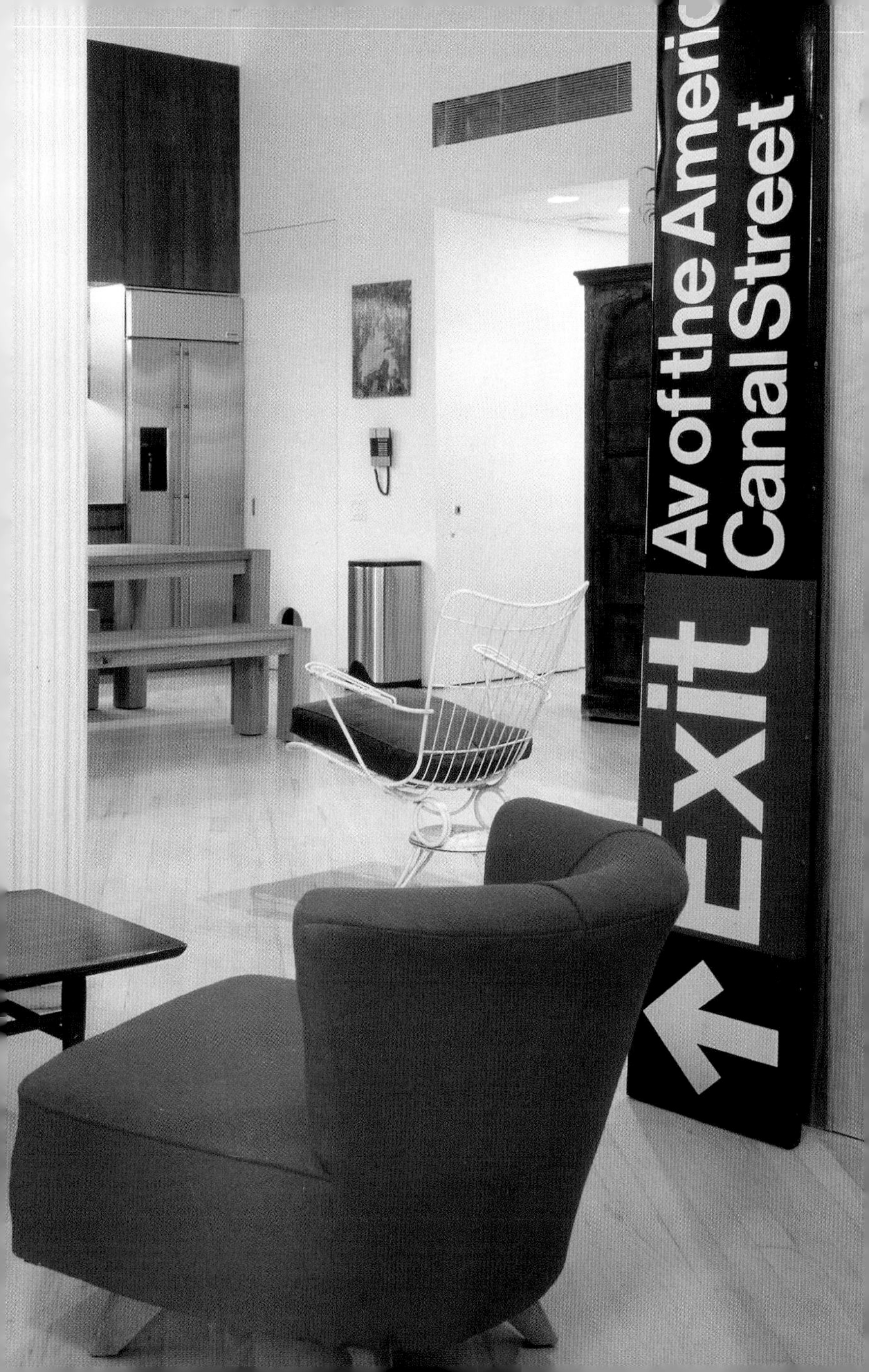
Av of the Americ
Canal Street
Exit

Beim Dekorieren und Möblieren des Wohnzimmers
dieser recht großen Wohnung entschied man sich
dazu, Möbel und Objekte zu verwenden, die
ebenfalls von beachtlicher Größe sind und somit
proportional zum Raum passen.

Because this living room has such ample
dimensions, it was decided to decorate it
accordingly. To achieve this, the furniture as
well as the objects used in its decoration are
of considerable proportions.

Au moment de décorer et meubler le salon de
ce logement de très grandes dimensions, on
a décidé d'utiliser des objets et un mobilier de
grande taille également, proportionnels au lieu.

Bij het inrichten en decoreren van de woonkamer
van deze grote woning werd gekozen voor grote
meubels en voorwerpen, in verhouding met de
ruimte.

Das Zimmerambiente wird durch die Farbe des Mobiliars und dadurch, wie sie mit Wänden und Boden kombiniert wird, bestimmt. Hier sind zwei sehr ungleiche Räume abgebildet, deren Möbel jedoch in den gleichen Farbtönen gehalten sind.

The ambiance of a room is defined by the color of its furnishings and how it combines with the walls and floor. Here we see two spaces that are completely different even though the furniture shares the same range of colors.

L'ambiance d'une pièce est définie par la couleur de son mobilier et par la combinaison avec les murs et le sol. On voit ici deux espaces totalement différents, même leurs meubles utilisent de la même gamme chromatique.

De sfeer in een vertrek wordt bepaald door de kleur van de meubels, en de combinatie ervan met de muren en vloer. Hier zien we twee compleet verschillende ruimtes, ondanks het meubilair in hetzelfde kleurgamma.

Essen und Trinken sind nicht mehr nur ein Grundbedürfnis, vielmehr haben sich in einen sozialen Akt verwandelt. Das Esszimmer ist der Ort, an dem Besucher empfangen werden, und sollte wie auch unsere Vorlieben beim Essen unseren Geschmack und unsere Persönlichkeit widerspiegeln.

More than a basic necessity, eating and drinking become a social event. The dining room has been selected to entertain our guests and it should reflect our taste and personality the same way that our gastronomic preferences do.

ETEN & DRINKEN

Plus qu'un besoin élémentaire, manger et boire est devenu un acte social. La salle à manger est le lieu choisi pour recevoir nos invités ; il doit refléter notre goût et notre personnalité, tout comme le font nos préférences gastronomiques.

Eten en drinken is niet zozeer een basisbehoefte, het is een sociaal gebeuren. In de eetkamer ontvangen we onze gasten. Ze geeft dus, net als onze gastronomische voorkeuren, uiting aan onze smaak en persoonlijkheid.

In Küchen, die genug Platz bieten, kann man einen Tisch stellen und somit die Mahlzeiten dort nicht nur zubereiten, sondern sie auch einnehmen. So entsteht ein entspanntes, intimes Ambiente.

Placing a table in kitchens where there is sufficient space, works well because it allows having meals in the kitchen in addition to cooking them. This creates a more relaxing and intimate atmosphere.

Dans les cuisines suffisamment grandes, il est possible de mettre une table, ce qui permet d'aménager cet espace pour prendre les repas en plus de les y préparer, ce qui donne une ambiance détendue et intime.

In voldoende ruime keukens is het mogelijk een tafel te plaatsen, waardoor in deze ruimte niet alleen kan worden gekookt, maar ook in alle rust en intimiteit kan worden gegeten.

In Wohnungen und Häusern mit offenen Räumen ist es möglich, das Essen verteilt zu servieren: der Aperitif auf den Sesseln im Wohnzimmer, und der Hauptgang je nach Raumaufteilung am Esszimmer-oder Küchentisch.

In homes where spaces are open, different meals can be served in different areas: appetizers can be eaten in the comfortable chairs of the living room while dinner is served in the kitchen or dining room.

Dans les logements où les espaces sont ouverts, on peut distribuer les activités : prendre l'apéritif dans les confortables fauteuils du salon et diner à la table de la salle à manger ou de la cuisine, selon la distribution.

In woningen met open ruimtes kan de maaltijd op verschillende plaatsen geserveerd worden: de borrel op een comfortabele bank in de zitkamer en het avondmaal in de keuken of eetkamer, afhankelijk van de indeling.

In diesem Raum wird ein kunstvolles Spiel aus Licht und Materialien erzeugt, bei dem kühle Farben wie Violett- und Blautöne verwendet wurden. Somit entsteht ein elegantes und avantgardistisches Ambiente.

The combinations of lights and colors in this room have been deliberately chosen. A palette of cold colors such as violet and different shades of blue has been used to create a modern, elegant space.

Dans cette pièce, on découvre un jeu de lumières et de matériaux étudié, où on a utilisé une palette de couleurs froides comprenant plusieurs tons de violet, de bleu, grâce à laquelle on créé un espace élégant et avant-gardiste.

In dit vertrek heerst een kunstig spel van licht en materialen, waarbij een koel kleurenpalet werd gebruikt, met violet en verschillende blauwtonen. Hierdoor ontstaat een stijlvolle en avant-gardistische ruimte.

Es gibt verschiedene Typen moderner Esszimmer, deren Dekoration vom Umfeld beeinflusst wird: links ein Esszimmer in einer ruhigen Ortschaft in Deutschland, und rechts das eines Apartments in der kosmopolitischen Stadt Shangai.

There are many types of modern dining rooms with decorations influenced by their surroundings. On the left, a home in a tranquil German location. On the right, an apartment in the cosmopolitan city of Shanghai.

Il existe plusieurs types de salles à manger, avec une décoration influencée par leur environnement : à gauche, celle d'une tranquille localité allemande et à droite, un appartement de la ville cosmopolite de Shangai.

Er zijn verschillende soorten moderne eetkamers, waarvan de decoratie inspiratie put uit de omgeving: links een woning in een rustig Duits stadje en rechts een appartement in de kosmopolitische stad Shangai.

Hier besteht keine aufwändige strukturelle Abgrenzung zwischen Küche und Esszimmer. Die Bereiche werden von einem Tisch abgegrenzt, der als Trennwand fungiert und für Aperitifs oder unförmliche Abendessen benutzt wird.

In this home there are no great structural separations between the kitchen and the dining room, so a table has been placed on the partition and can be used to serve appetizers or informal dinners.

Dans ce logement, il n'existe pas de grandes séparations entre la cuisine et la salle à manger. C'est la table, montée dans une cloison, qui divise les espaces et sert aux apéritifs ou aux diners informels.

In deze woning zijn de keuken en eetkamer niet volledig van elkaar gescheiden. Tussen beide ruimtes staat een tafel die fungeert als scheidingswand en gebruikt wordt voor een aperitief of informeel etentje.

Der Zen-Stil, eine der derzeit avantgardistischsten Tendenzen, zeichnet sich, wie man hier sieht, durch die Verwendung natürlicher Materialien, schlichte Linien und die Abschaffung aller oberflächlichen und unnötigen Elemente aus.

Le style zen, une des tendances les plus avant-gardiste, se caractérise par l'utilisation de matériaux naturels, de lignes simples et par la suppression de tout élément superficiel ou superflu, comme on le voit dans cette pièce.

Zen is one of the more modern styles and is mostly characterized by the use of natural materials, simple lines and for suppressing superficial and unnecessary elements as can be appreciated in this room.

Dit vertrek is een goed voorbeeld van de zenstijl, een van de meest avant-gardistische huidige trends, gekenmerkt door natuurlijke materialen, eenvoudige lijnen en het ontbreken van oppervlakkige en onnodige elementen.

Der Minimalismus dieser Küche vermischt sich mit der barocken Eleganz der über dem Tisch hängenden Lampe.Links ist ein Raum abgebildet, der die gleiche Funktion hat, aber sehr anders, wesentlich klassischer und rustikaler wirkt.

The minimalism in the kitchen mixes with the baroque elegance of the lamp in the dining room. On the left we see a space whose function is the same and yet the aspect is totally different; much more classic and rural.

Le minimalisme de la cuisine se mêle à l'élégance baroque de la lampe de la salle à manger. A gauche, on découvre un espace qui remplit la même fonction et offre un aspect totalement différent, beaucoup plus classique et rural.

Dit is een mengeling van een minimalistische keuken met een stijlvolle, barokke lamp boven de tafel. Links zien we een ruimte die dezelfde functie heeft en er helemaal anders uitziet, veel klassieker en landelijker.

Bei diesem Raum, in dem Wohn- und Esszimmer untergebracht sind, dominiert das Schwarz der Möbel. Von daher wurden bei der Dekoration kleine Farbdetails aufgenommen, die den Raum gemütlicher wirken lassen.

Dans ce grand espace, qui accueille le salon et la salle à manger, domine le noir du mobilier ; on a donc introduit les petites touches de couleur des éléments décoratifs, qui aident à rendre la pièce plus accueillante.

In this ample space that houses the living room and dining room, the black of the furniture is quite dominating, so color has been introduced through decorative elements. These color details make the atmosphere cozier.

In deze grote ruimte, waarin zich een zit- en eetkamer bevinden, overheerst het zwart van de meubels. Een vleugje kleur in de decoratieve elementen maakt de ruimte gezelliger.

Seit Jahrtausenden schon weiß man um den Zusammenhang zwischen Schlaf und körperlichem Wohlbefinden. Während des Schlafs ruhen Körper und Geist und tanken Kraft, um dem neuen Tag entgegen treten zu können. Deshalb ist der Ort, an dem wir schlafen, sehr wichtig. All seine Elemente beeinflussen uns, vom Bett bis hin zu den Farben und Materialien, die uns umgeben.

Sleep has always been related to the physical wellbeing of people. It is the time our minds and bodies use to recover and prepare for the following day. For this reason, the place where we sleep is very important, as is the selection of bed-type, colors and surrounding materials.

SLAAPKAMERS

Pendant des millénaires, dormir a été lié au bien-être physique des personnes. C'est le moment où notre corps et notre esprit se reposent et reprennent des forces pour affronter une nouvelle journée. Pour cela, le lieu où nous dormons est très important et nous influence, du choix du type de lit, aux couleurs et aux matériaux qui nous entourent.

Sinds mensenheugenis wordt slapen met welzijn geassocieerd. Als we slapen rusten ons lichaam en onze geest, en laden we onze batterij op om klaar te zijn voor een nieuwe dag. Daarom is de plek waar we slapen heel belangrijk en kiezen we zorgvuldig het soort bed, de kleuren en materialen die ons omringen.

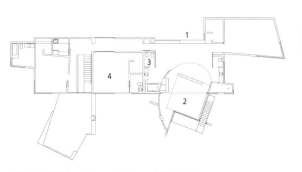

1. Entree
2. Slaapkamer
3. Badkamer
4. Woonkamer

Plattegrond die de ronding van het slaapgedeelte laat zien.

1. Entree
2. Woonkamer
3. Badkamer
4. Keuken
5. Slaapkamer
6. Badkamer
7. Slaapkamer

Begane grond

1. Entree
2. Keuken
3. Eetkamer
4. Woonkamer
5. Badkamer
6. Trap

Begane grond

Begane grond
Om de ruimte zo optimaal mogelijk te benutten, is de slaapkamer
op een andere verdieping.

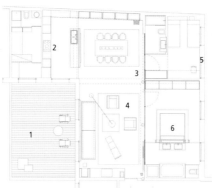

1. Entree
2. Keuken
3. Eetkamer
4. Woonkamer
5. Slaapkamer
6. Slaapkamer

Begane grond

1. Entree
2. Badkamer
3. Keuken
4. Woonkamer
5. Entree slaapkamer
6. Slaapkamer

Plattegrond die laat zien dat het slaapgedeelte een aparte ruimte is in huis.

1. Woonkamer
2. Slaapkamer
3. Badkamer
4. Keuken
5. Eetkamer

Plattegrond penthouse

Kinderzimmer zeichnen sich durch ihre Farbgestaltung aus. Früher wurden sie in Himmelblau und Rosa gestaltet, aber gegenwärtig werden kräftigere Farben wie Gelb-, Rot- und Grüntöne bevorzugt. Neue Materialien, fröhliche Formen und ein Meer aus Farben bieten große Vielfalt bei der Erschaffung verschiedener Ambiente, in denen Kinder ihren Fantasien freien Lauf lassen können.

Children's rooms stand out for their colors. In the past, they were full of blues and pinks, but today, stronger shades are used, such as yellows, reds, and greens. New materials, cheerful forms and a full array of colors offer a great variety of atmospheres where children can play out their fantasies.

KINDERKAMERS

Les chambres d'enfants se remarquent par leurs couleurs. Avant, on les couvrait de bleu ciel et de rose, mais aujourd'hui les tons plus vifs, comme les jaunes, les rouges ou les verts, trouvent leur place. Les nouveaux matériaux, les formes joyeuses et ce déluge de couleurs offrent une grande variété d'ambiances, où les enfants laissent libre cours à toutes leurs fantaisies.

Kinderkamers vallen op door hun kleuren. Vroeger werd vooral lichtblauw of roze gebruikt, maar tegenwoordig is er ook plaats voor fellere kleuren, zoals geel, rood of groen. Nieuwe materialen, vrolijke vormen en een ruim kleurenpalet bieden ontelbare mogelijkheden om de kinderfantasie de vrije loop te laten.

Auch bei Kinderzimmern kann man dekorative Tendenzen vernehmen. Dieses Kinderzimmer, in dem klare Linien und die Farbe Weiß, die mit zarten Grün-, Lila- und Rottönen kombiniert wurde, ist minimalistisch angehaucht.

On peut également observer les tendances décoratives dans les chambres des enfants. Dans cette chambre minimaliste, les lignes simples et le blanc, qui se mêlent ici aux verts, mauves et roses délicats, sont omniprésents.

Decoration tendencies can also be appreciated in children's playrooms and bedrooms. In this one, we see hints of minimalism with pure lines and white which has been combined with greens, pinks and lilacs.

Kinderkamers geven ook uiting aan decoratieve trends. In deze minimalistische slaapkamer overheersen eenvoudige lijnen en wit, hier in combinatie met lichtgroen, lila en roze.

123

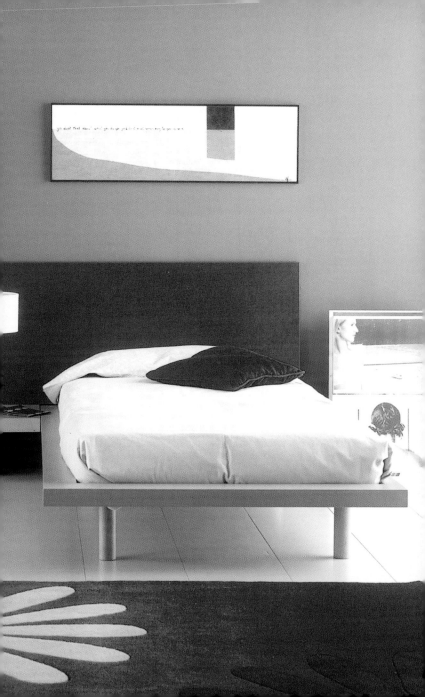

Tiere sind ein geläufiges Motiv in den Kinderzimmern von Jungen und Mädchen. Das Motiv taucht in Bildern, als Aufdruck der Bettwäsche oder in Form von Stofftieren in den verschiedensten Größen und Materialien auf.

Animals have always been a recurrent theme in boy's as well as girl's bedrooms. They are used in pictures and paintings, stuffed toys of various shapes and sizes, and printed on sheet sets and comforters.

Les animaux ont toujours été un thème récurrent dans les chambres des petits enfants. Ils apparaissent en peintures, sur les imprimés des draps et des couettes ou sous forme de peluches de différentes tailles et matériaux.

Dierenmotieven komen vaak voor in zowel jongens- als meisjeskamers. Ze worden gebruikt in schilderijen, bedrukte lakens, dekbedden en knuffels in verschillende grootes en materialen.

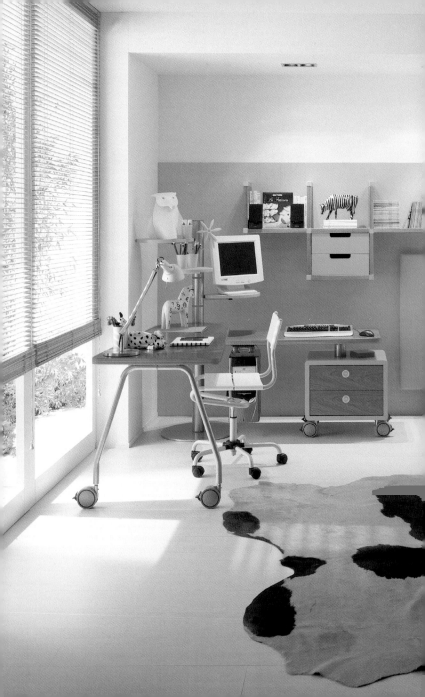

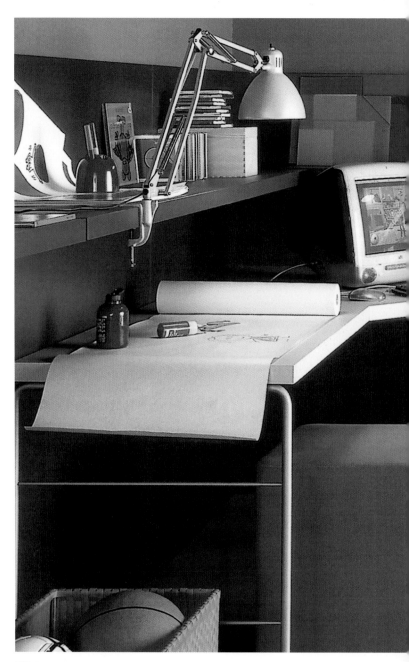

Zu Hause haben Erwachsene das gleiche Recht zu spielen wie Kinder. In diesem Sinne wird versucht, den Stressabbau und eine maximale Ausnutzung der Freizeit zu Hause zu unterstützen. Für einige bedeutet das, ein Instrument zu spielen, für andere, Sport zu treiben und für manche, Filme in Kinoatmosphäre anzusehen.

In the home, adults have as much right to play as children do. We look for ways to leave stress behind and maximize the spare time at home. For some, it may be playing a musical instrument, while for others it might be a full workout, and still, others might just want to enjoy a movie as they would in the theatre.

ONTSPANNINGSRUIMTEN

À la maison, les adultes ont, comme les enfants, le droit de jouer. Pour cela, on cherche des façons de se défaire du stress et de profiter au mieux du temps libre que l'on passe à la maison. Pour certains, cela signifie jouer d'un instrument, pour d'autres faire de l'exercice et d'autres apprécient un film dans les conditions du cinéma.

Ook volwassenen hebben, net als kinderen, recht op ontspanning. Daarom gaan we op zoek naar manieren om de stress te vergeten en onze vrije tijd thuis maximaal te benutten. Voor de een is dit een muziekinstrument bespelen, voor de ander beweging nemen, en voor nog weer een ander genieten van een film alsof ze in de bioscoop zitten.

G L A D I A T O R
PLAY MOVIE
SCENE SELECTIONS
SUBTITLES
LANGUAGES/AUDIO SET UP

In dieses Wohnzimmer hat man eine große Leinwand integriert, die zur Projektion von Filmen benutzt wird, und dabei über eine Fernbedienung leicht bedient werden kann. Sie holt den Zauber des Kinos nach Hause.

In the living room of this home, a big screen has been installed to project movies and bring the magic of the theatre into the home. It can be easily concealed by the touch of a remote control button.

Dans le salon de ce logement, a été installé un grand écran utilisé pour projeter des film, et qui se range très facilement grâce à une télécommande, et grâce auquel on fait entrer la magie du cinéma à la maison.

Een groot scherm in de zitkamer, dat met een afstandbediening kan worden opgeborgen, is als een bioscoop in huis.

Bei diesem Raum steht das audiovisuelle Erlebnis im Vordergrund. Hierzu wurden über den weitläufigen Raum verteilt mehrere Hightech-Geräte wie HiFi-Anlagen, Verstärker, Projektoren und ein gigantischer Bildschirm aufgebaut.

Dans cette pièce, on cherche à vivre l'expérience audiovisuelle. On a donc installé dans ce bel espace, plusieurs appareils de haute technologie comme les chaines hifi, des amplis, des projecteurs et un écran géant.

This room is meant for audiovisual enjoyment. To achieve this, advanced technology equipment such as sound transmitters, amplifiers, projectors and a giant screen have been installed in the ample space.

Deze kamer is gericht op audiovisueel genieten. Ze is voorzien van verschillende geluidsinstallaties, versterkers en een gigantisch scherm.

In Spielzimmern, die ausreichend Platz bieten, um einen großen Tisch aufzustellen, sind Spiele wie Tischtennis und Billard eine gute Alternative, da sowohl Kinder als auch Erwachsene an ihnen Freude haben.

In game rooms where there is sufficient space to allow a big table, ping-pong and pool are good alternatives to be considered. Adults as well as children of different ages can enjoy these two timeless games.

Dans les salles de jeux où l'espace est suffisamment grand pour installer une table, le ping-pong et le billard sont une bonne option, car les enfants comme les adultes l'utilisent.

Spelletjes als tafeltennis en biljart zijn een goed idee voor een speelkamer die ruim genoeg is om er een tafel in te plaatsen, want klein en groot genieten ervan.

Mit Höchstgeschwindigkeit durch Indianapolis heizen oder in einem Helikopter fliegen, sind Erlebnisse, die mit diesem an einen großen Wandbildschirm angeschlossenen Videospielautomaten virtuell wahr werden.

Speed racing in Indianapolis, navigating a yacht, or flying a helicopter are all experiences within easy reach – virtually – thanks to this game-chair that connects to a great screen installed on the wall.

Piloter un bolide à Indianapolis, un bateau ou un hélicoptère, sont des expériences qui peuvent être réalisées – virtuellement – grâce à ce fauteuil de jeux, connecté à un grand écran accroché au mur.

Deze spelletjesstoel, die aangesloten is op een groot scherm aan de muur, maakt het mogelijk virtueel te racen in Indianapolis of te vliegen met een helikopter.

Ob es regnet oder schneit, ein klimatisiertes Schwimmbecken im Haus ermöglicht zu jeder Jahreszeit Badespaß. Es wird immer gebräuchlicher, dass dabei die Beheizung des Wassers über Solarzellen stattfindet.

Qu'il pleuve ou qu'il neige dehors, une piscine intérieure climatisée permet de se baigner en toute saison. Il est de plus en plus fréquent que cette climatisation soit faite par l'intermédiaire de panneaux solaires.

Swimming can take place at any time of the year without worrying about rain or snow when there is an interior temperature controlled swimming pool. It is more and more common that these pools are heated by solar power.

Regen of sneeuw beletten ons niet het hele jaar door een frisse duik te nemen in een verwarmd binnenzwembad. Steeds vaker worden zwembaden verwarmd door middel van zonnepanelen.

Heutzutage haben die meisten Häuser und Wohnungen ein Arbeitszimmer. Der Raum, den wir als Büro nutzen, beeinflusst direkt unsere Konzentrationsfähigkeit und unsere Arbeitseffizienz. Von daher ist es fundamental, dass dieser Raum hell und leise ist. Bei der Dekoration ist es besonders wichtig, dass die verschiedenen Formen, Farben und Materialien auf einander abgestimmt werden.

Today, most homes have an office. The space we use as an office has a direct impact on our ability to concentrate, and our work efficiency, which is why it is important to have a quiet, well-lighted area. To decorate it, we should consider a balance of form, color and material.

WERKRUIMTEN

Aujourd'hui, la majorité des foyers disposent d'un bureau. L'espace que nous utilisons comme bureau influence directement notre capacité de concentration et notre efficacité au travail ; il est donc fondamental qu'il s'agisse d'un lieu lumineux et silencieux. Pour le décorer, le plus important est d'équilibrer correctement les formes, les couleurs et les matériaux.

Vandaag de dag beschikken de meeste huizen over een werkkamer. De ruimte die we als kantoor gebruiken beïnvloedt rechtstreeks ons concentratievermogen en of we al dan niet efficiënt werken. Vandaar dat het een stille plek, met veel licht moet zijn. Bij de decoratie dienen vormen, kleuren en materialen goed in evenwicht te zijn.

1. & 2. Studio
3. Entree
4. Tweede verdieping
5. Eerste verdieping
6. Trap
7. Trap
8. Opstand
9. Façade

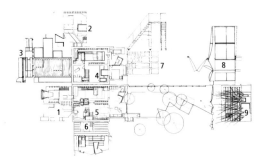

Plattegrond

Verhoging zuidkant en dwarsdoorsnede.

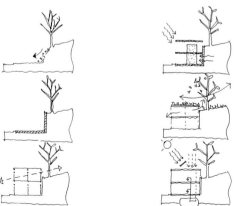

Opbouw van de constructie, volledig opgenomen in de omgeving.

237

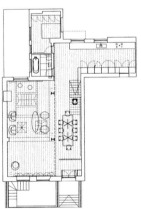

Bovenste verdieping, waar het kantoor zich bevindt.

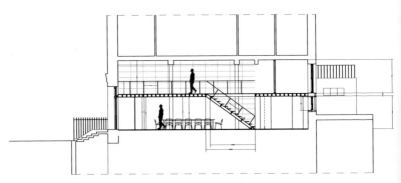

Dwarsdoorsnede die de route door het huis aangeeft.

Der als Arbeitszimmer genutzte Raum wurde wie
ein kleines, unabhängiges Haus konzipiert, das
sich auf einer Schiebeplattform befindet. Wird sie
zur Seite geschoben, öffnet sich eine Fläche, die
man als Garten nutzen kann.

The area designated for the office space in this
home, has been built as a small, independent
house and has been mounted on a moving
platform. When moved, the available space can
be used as a garden.

L'espace destiné au bureau de cette résidence a
été conçu comme une petite maison indépendante,
monté sur une plate-forme coulissante. En la
déplaçant, elle laisse un espace ouvert qui peut
être utilisé comme jardin.

Het kantoor in deze woning ligt op een
schuifplatform en werd gebouwd als een apart
huis. Als het platform verschoven wordt, is er
een open ruimte die als tuin kan worden
gebruikt.

FOTOVERANTWOORDING